♥ ♥ ♥ ♥ ♥ ♥ ♥

HEART TO HEART

ELAINE CANNON

Bookcraft · Salt Lake City, Utah

Copyright © 1983 by Bookcraft, Inc.

Library of Congress Catalog Card Number 83-72680
ISBN 0-88494-505-7

2 3 4 5 6 7 8 9 10   89 88 87 86 85 84

Lithographed in the United States of America
PUBLISHERS PRESS
Salt Lake City, Utah

HEART
TO
HEART

CONTENTS

ABOUT HEART TO HEART

This collection is called
Heart to Heart because it is about some of the
things that make all the quality difference in
your heart, in your life.

Heart to heart, back and forth from me to
you; and because I have learned so much
through you, from you to me. Back and forth
flow the feelings, the ideas, the perspective, the
life-lifting lessons, the glistening things. Heart to
heart—an exchange of truth, goodness, sense,
simple steps, and loveliness.

The heart is the center of the soul, the
tender core of a person's whole being. When we
look to the center of ourself—to the heart—we
find something lovely emerging, like the butterfly
from its cocoon.

The heart sometimes knows what the mind
can't explain yet. The heart surges, bursts, swells,
warms, melts, burns, knows, remembers! The
heart, graphically speaking, is the symbol of the
center of us, of Life and Love. And it is the
promising place: hand over heart to tell the
truth, to declare honor, to signal sincerity, to
pledge allegiance, to share solemn secrets, to
hold tight sacred moments.

The heart is the significant place. Consider
these phrases from great literature and scripture:
When the heart speaks it needs no preparation
...that which cometh from the heart will go to

the heart . . . an understanding heart . . . blessed are the pure in heart . . . knit your hearts with an unslipping knot . . . the heart hath its own memory, like the mind, and in it are enshrined the precious keepsakes.

Tennyson summed it up this way for you,

> "Brave hearts and clean! yet—
> God guide them! young—"

Heart to Heart is for very special people.

from Elaine Cannon

ABOUT YOUR HEART

Have a heart... think
of yourself. Following the dictates of your own
conscience can save some heartache. Melissa
went to the movies with a boy she'd long
wanted to impress, to be friends with. It was
great fun until the film was well under way, and
then there flashed across the screen some scenes
she felt were inappropriate for public sharing.
She winced and felt a little sick inside, but she
wanted to keep in the good graces of the group.
Besides, she needed a ride home. What to do?
She looked into her heart, so to speak, and
decided to go out into the lobby until the show
was over. After she had been gone a time, her
boyfriend began to worry and went out to find
her. He admitted he'd been embarrassed, too.
Together they waited for the rest of the group.
Curious and concerned, the others came out one
by one. Because one girl looked into her own
heart and dared to take a stand on her own,
others had the courage to follow.

In your own settings, in your own way, you
can be the gentle, unjudgmental example of
doing what is right by doing what is right. One's
heart is one's conscience, it is the guiding center
from God. Jeremiah 17:7-8 reminds us: "Blessed
is the [one] that trusteth in the Lord, and whose
hope the Lord is. For [she] shall be as a tree
planted by the waters, and that spreadeth out

her roots by the river, and shall not see when heat cometh, but her leaf shall be green; and shall not be careful in the year of drought, neither shall cease from yielding fruit."

In the sixth chapter of Proverbs we read: "These six things doth the Lord hate: yea, seven are an abomination unto him: A proud look, a lying tongue, and hands that shed innocent blood, *An heart that deviseth wicked imaginations,* feet that be swift in running to mischief, a false witness that speaketh lies, and he that soweth discord."

What about your heart?

Here are some qualities I want to fill my heart with:

_____

_____

_____

_____

_____

_____

_____

_____

_____

_____

_____

_____

_____

_____

_____

_____

_____

_____

_____

_____

_____

_____

_____

_____

_____

♥　♥　♥　♥　♥　♥　♥

ABOUT DESTINY

*I*t's a mobile world, and somebody is always going someplace. Some people pray for safety before a trip. In the home of one family who always paused for prayer before the car was started, the young son was called on to pray. Little Briton uttered these wise words, "Heavenly Father, please help us get safely to our destiny." He meant destination, of course, but the slip of a child's tongue teaches the rest of us. Shouldn't such a prayer constantly fill the heart of each of us—that we'll reach our destiny whole and wholesome?

To give life meaning, we need a focus, a goal, a reason for being, a purpose, a destiny. Matthew Arnold was right when he wrote, "Such a price the Gods exact for song: to become what we sing."

Thoreau, you recall, went to the woods so that he might live life deliberately, with a certain control and with time to think. Paul explained to the Corinthians that we see through a glass darkly when we think and understand only as a child might. If we want to meet our own particular destiny, we must be certain we are on the path that will lead us there. We need to do some very careful thinking, learning, choosing, living.

Five years from now I'd like to have accomplished the following:

_____

_____

_____

_____

_____

_____

_____

_____

_____

_____

_____

_____

_____

_____

_____

_____

_____

_____

_____

_____

_____

_____

_____

_____

♥ ♥ ♥ ♥ ♥ ♥ ♥

ABOUT LIVING
MORE HAPPILY

*F*ocus on your future
Eternity is forever, and happiness there is worth
  disciplining yourself for now.

Plot your plans
Learn the requirements to meet your goals—and
  live accordingly.

Follow the Master's plan
It's all there. It's all for you. And it's for real.

Love your family
Tender, loving interest works wonders both
  ways.

Do unto others as you'd have others do unto
  you
That's what personal appeal comes down to.

Watch the advance notices
Even you'll have to cope with temptation, so
  keep your eyes open, your answers ready,
  and your resolves strong.

Repeat after me a hundred times
Honesty *is* the best policy. (You'll see, in a
  hundred different ways!)

Know yourself
And learn the importance of having integrity in
  all your actions, all your thoughts, all your
  dealings with your friends and with your
  God.

Here are some people who have helped me live more happily:

_____
_____
_____
_____
_____
_____
_____
_____
_____
_____
_____
_____
_____
_____
_____
_____
_____
_____
_____
_____
_____
_____
_____
_____
_____
_____
_____

♥ ♥ ♥ ♥ ♥ ♥ ♥

ABOUT BRIGHT IDEAS

*I*t's a bright idea

to get your light out from under that proverbial
   bushel (read Matthew 5:15-16 once more in
   terms of *you*).

to dream dreams and make wishes, remembering
   that your Aladdin's lamp is your willingness
   to work to make things come true.

to hitch your wagon to a star; to look heaven-
   ward; to think big; to climb high; to cultivate
   the upward reach.

to admit that Jesus wants you for a sunbeam,
   too. He needs teens as well as toddlers to
   light the way for others.

to flash your smile upon those you meet. Watch
   their faces light up, too.

to realize that the moon has many moods, many
   faces. (So have you!) Each one is lovely.
   (Are yours?)

to let the warmth of your hearth spread the
   warmth of your heart. Popcorn and people
   and firelight spell fun and good memories.

to be in tune with youth; to take uncommon
   pleasure in common things.

to look for good in everyone—specifically logging
   it in your consciousness.

to feel your heart grow through little givings.

to blessing count.

to organize the mementos of cheerful yesterdays into a treasure for all the tomorrows.

to feel wonder, awe, humility, in the face of the span of life.

to search for beauty and find it in surprising places.

to confidently know what's out and what's in— like the tide.

to be selective about new trends, new tendencies.

to remember what's right and what's not right, according to God.

to discover the sudden sweetness of silence and self.

to read, to respond as words from an oft-read page suddenly leap out to your heart with new meaning.

to awaken to the fantastic effectiveness of the Golden Rule—so simple you almost miss the point.

to remember you only live one round. No time for foolishness. No time to reinvent the wheel.

And it's a bright idea

to remember when summer was synonymous with sandpiles.

to remember when the "school's-out" shout meant long weeks building tents in the yard, playing dolls in the orchard, having dance lessons in the neighbor's basement, opening lemonade stands, picking berries, exploring the local hills.

But . . . You've done a lot to change all that. You've grown up.

And now in summer you are caught up in the wonderful world of a mobile generation. You're on the move. You go—here, there, and across the seas. You ride and sail and sight-see. It may be just for fun. Or if you're one of the lucky ones, you work some, too. You're so busy you're breathless.

In the midst of it all, there ought to be time enough to think about where it is you really are going and how you are getting there and what you'll be like when you arrive. You could make summer synonymous with scripture study, soul searching, goal setting for personal progress, and be better than ever.

Becoming a woman lays a lovely cloak upon you—a cloak of refinement, individuality, personal choice, and responsibility. And great reward.

It is a very bright idea to get on with good growing from a bud into a bloom.

Here are some of my own bright ideas:

♥   ♥   ♥   ♥   ♥   ♥   ♥

ABOUT PARENTS AND PLEASANTNESS

Making friends with the family is important. Being pleasant with your parents brings its own reward. Families are the basis of life.

Families are very personal. Yours is different from someone else's family. You have more in common, for one thing. You know things about each other that "outsiders" don't. You've already shared the traditions, the beginnings, the growings, the sicknesses, the disasters, the heartbreak, the crop failures, the floods, the quarrels even. And along the way there has been love, because that's how a family came to be in the first place. Loving and pleasantness are related and need to be nurtured.

Sometimes unhappiness begins at home because teenagers suddenly see that parents aren't perfect. They seem to have changed from the ideal folks they knew as children. They now seem to be a bundle of shortcomings.

Parents often look at teenagers as different, too—no longer as trusting and innocent children. Parents see their darling child suddenly a stranger in their paradise. They feel you have changed from one who loved them and needed them to one who is independent, a mystery, perhaps a problem. Sometimes each gets verbal in this transition. Each begins to find fault in everything the other does.

Home is no place for a battleground. War never solved any problems, really. Pleasantness as a fact in your home can help people to be patient while each grows toward better understanding of the other and adjusts to a new view.

You grow inches in a summer, but parents don't seem to have changed since your childhood. Let them catch up with your new look, new abilities. Help keep them current by telling, sharing, showing, without making them feel like has-beens (that's so deflating!).

You may rebel at feeling owned, at being ordered, advised, or disciplined at your age. Parents feel a sense of duty—and it's a fact they're legally and morally responsible for you.

Parents are your best blessing. They *care*. They're the people who love you—anyway. And you are all in this family thing together. It's a strange quirk of the system, but while you may think they're disappointed in you, *they* may feel they've failed you. Your family may not be as rich as you'd like or as active in the Church, or maybe they quarrel too much; but they are your family just the same, and there isn't anything you can do about *that*. But there is much you can do about the *quality* of your relationships.

Pleasantness is next to godliness, and since God has based his peopling of the universe on families, since God has decreed that growing up for parents and youth happens best in the family setting, why not try pleasantness?

You can start it. You don't have to be a parent to be pleasant.

Finding a good solution to any teen-parent block is well worth the trouble. While the difficulty may last for only a few years usually, still those very years are most important in determining family patterns for the years to come.

Heaven at home is a pleasant possibility when everybody tries.

My parents are great because:

_____
_____
_____
_____
_____
_____
_____
_____
_____
_____
_____
_____
_____
_____
_____
_____
_____
_____
_____
_____
_____
_____
_____
_____
_____
_____
_____
_____
_____

ABOUT FINDING TIME

Oh, would that I could find the time
To do a deed for self, sublime!
A quiet time, a secret place
I'd look inside, behind my face
To find the best that's deep in me
To recognize what God can see.
My inner soul could gently guide
The things I do as on I stride.
I'd be kinder day by day
More careful in the things I say
Then chanted verse would turn to truth—
The life I live would be truth's proof.
But I'm so busy; pressures mount
So much to do I cannot count.
Oh, would that I could find the time
To do a deed for self, sublime!

Here is how I organize my time:

_____

_____

_____

_____

_____

_____

_____

_____

_____

_____

_____

_____

_____

_____

_____

_____

_____

_____

_____

_____

_____

_____

_____

_____

_____

_____

_____

_____

ABOUT DOING WHAT'S RIGHT

*T*here is a wonderful old hymn which rouses a Christian congregation during the chorus: "Do what is right, let the consequence follow." It's one to memorize. It's a song to sing in the trying times of temptation and decision. It's a stirring sound—a kind of crutch in time of need.

Sing! Sing the reminder to do what is right and believe the line about "God will protect you."

Save yourself from doing what's wrong.

Consider the case of Julie.

Julie was one of the prettiest girls in her teenage group—pretty but pitiful, as it turned out. Julie let herself get caught in a kind of terrible trap. She failed to do what is right. As the weeks passed, the tears and fears were well based. Who needs a baby when you're barely through being one yourself? But Julie was caught —pretty, pitiful Julie.

What then must she do?

Barrels of tears—weeping and wailing and gnashing of teeth is the way the scriptures describe such remorse—but tears don't make it all go away.

Julie had been disobedient. She had given in to temptation, given in to nature's drive without giving obedient attention to God, creator of all nature, and his regulations for procreation. Julie was a child of God who had broken God's law. The baby on its way was the innocent spirit child of God. Should it be punished for Julie's failure to do what was right?

What then must Julie do? Take hasty legal action called marriage? Have an abortion? Keep the baby and let mom and dad help rear the child?

Two wrongs don't make a right.

Wisely counseled at last, Julie retreated from her familiar world for a time; she withdrew from being a poor example to her peers and the object of gossip by her presence. Since marriage to the young man was not possible, she wisely gave up the baby for adoption into a loving, established family who could give it all the advantages Julie couldn't right then.

Nobody said it was easy, but it was doing what is right; it was knowing God will at last forgive and bless. Sacrifice and faith, repentance and restitution and courage are what we're talking about here.

Later Julie finished high school and went on to get a wonderful job following business school. And, no doubt, one of these days she will fall in love—real love, not curious lust—and be married and be a mother, too.

Julie learned to keep close to the Lord through all her ups and downs in life and to feel his redeeming love.

Hopefully, you'll never be a Julie with that kind of heartbreak, but it's a good thing to remember that if you have a problem, solving it the Lord's way is the best way. That is doing what's right when you've done wrong.

My favorite scriptures on repentance:

_____

_____

_____

_____

_____

_____

_____

_____

_____

_____

_____

_____

_____

_____

_____

_____

_____

_____

_____

_____

_____

_____

_____

_____

_____

ABOUT HONOR

The great ones have had much to say about honor. Reciting a pledge, expressing a creed, making a promise with the phrase "on my honor," therein is lofty business, a beautiful pursuit, a noble aim. But saying so doesn't make it so. Doing does.

Honor operates in your life through an inner determination of the will to do what seems good and right to you under the circumstances—no matter what! Your conscience is your guide; a sense of shame and varying torment is your punishment for acting against your sense of honor, falling short of your own ideal.

Honor is more than duty. It is more than self-respect. It is better than the praise of men. It is more than Aristotle's "highmindedness." It goes beyond virtue and rules out vanity. It couples with courage. To be honorable is to be godly. To be godly is our ultimate aim, our promise of maximum happiness.

Did you ever consider: What it really means when you vow, "I give you my word of honor..." What kind of promise you are making when you recite, "On my honor I will..." What kind of effort is needed if you are to "graduate with honors." What kind of special behavior is required if you are to keep God's commandment to "Honour thy father and thy mother."

Here are some lessons about honor that I've learned through Church, school, family life, reading, or personal experience:

_____
_____
_____
_____
_____
_____
_____
_____
_____
_____
_____
_____
_____
_____
_____
_____
_____
_____
_____
_____
_____
_____
_____
_____
_____

ABOUT RELATING
TO OTHERS

Treat others as you like to be treated

The Golden Rule works. The parables tell
the story. The results of such living are in the
miracle class. The Golden Rule works. Honesty,
compassion, comfort, loyalty, concern, and
a big effort to keep things pleasant are principles
involved here.

Care and be aware

Remember names and remember the facts.
Put the two together at the right time. Keep up
with and make comments on what friends are
doing. Encourage, compliment when a compliment is due, hold sacred the confidences, and go
easy on the criticism.

Smile

Smile. Smile. Smile. But not pointlessly.
Smile at someone with an eye-to-eye approach.
Make the contact. Connect. A smile is the
nicest way to touch and be touched in the
friendly interplay of personalities.

Relating to your relations

Here are some ideas out of many that you
can do so you'll come to know your own relations... like them as well as love them, and have
some joy in accomplishment.

Have a reunion

The meaning of that phrase is "get together again." Send out a brown bag labeled a "blessing bag" and inside put an invitation to come and blessing count about how great it is to be related. Suggest assignments for each cousin. Refreshment is an assignment, but so is a newsletter with information about what everyone is doing. So are name tags. So is a list of "blessings" to go in everyone's bag, such as a copy of your family tree, a short history of some colorful relative.

Swap photos

Set a date and have a relating-to-relations photo swap. If everyone brings copies of family pictures, you can make a marvelous collage. Duplicate copies or make poster-size blow-ups for anyone willing to pay. Be sure to remind your cousins to put identification on each picture.

Relating to friends

Friends are a source of great happiness. A true friend likes you anyway. A friend is a bit of excitement along the way. Getting along great with your friends is a skill worth cultivating. It's so much *fun*! Follow the golden rules of the good books on human relationships and you'll be glad you did. Here are three ideas for you to consider for three kinds of friendship in your young life:

You're a twosome

Hurrah! Having found each other, keep your relationship rich by going places and doing things that inspire searching talk and quiet thought. A country walk, a sacred or historical spot, some good music.

Mix-match groups

Play casts, youth committees, or other structured associations require special preparations for likable togetherness. Have a sing-along, redecorate a room at the church, stage a talent hour, but bring along simple popcorn in a basket, cookies in bright paper sacks, fruit in home-sewn calico bags.

Gatherings

When serving your menu try to make the food look exciting as well as taste great. And pick the people for the party with the same kind of care.

My very own Ten Commandments for happy relationships:

ABOUT BOYS

*T*hey forget your birth-day. They're shy about dates. If there isn't a game, they just might go to the dance. They tease in the halls—though it's fun just the same—when they call on the phone they act as if they can't remember your name.

Give them a chance
and they will
eat
eat
eat
eat
eat
all of your chocolate-chip cookies.
That's the truth about boys.

More About Boys

It's time for your date.
Your hair doesn't "work"
There's a blemish in sight
Your retainer hurts
Your crying is a blight
It's puffing your eyes
Life is the pits
And you wish you could die.
Then *he* comes to the door
His smile says you look great
Bless him!—You smile back
It'll be a fun date.

About Brothers

"It isn't fair," the girl said with dismay,
"You got the curly hair and the straight nose."
"But, Sis," he replied, "It's okay. Don't you see?
You got the straight hair and the curly nose?"

These are the boys/men I like best and the reasons why:

_____

_____

_____

_____

_____

_____

_____

_____

_____

_____

_____

_____

_____

_____

_____

_____

_____

_____

_____

_____

_____

_____

_____

_____

_____

_____

_____

ABOUT EYES THAT SEE

On the move? Half the world is. Wherever you travel you take a bit of your home with you. You take something of your church and much of your family. No one is perfect, we all are quick to admit, but trying to be perfect helps. For a traveler, good intentions are good beginnings.

1. Leave your "Halloween costumes" at home and take proper city clothes for city places, resort clothes for resorts.

2. Don't criticize the local territory to the natives. It's their homeland, and they like it.

3. The language of a gracious smile needs no translation in any country. That goes for gracious behavior, too.

4. Plan time on your itinerary for basic grooming needs so that you don't appear as one of the not-so-scenic sights.

5. Talk with people, drink in the culture, taste the strange new foods, and learn all you can.

6. "Be thou an example of the believers, in word, in conversation, in charity, in spirit, in faith, in purity" (1 Timothy 4:12).

7. Have eyes that truly see.

Youthful Vision

Do you
have
20/20 vision
about God
and your life and about
the people you live with
and
the school you attend
and the places you go and
the
things you do and
the clothes you wear and
the parties you
give
and the city you live in
and its laws and its
customs and its
beauties
about the church you belong to
and its standards
and principles
and blessings
and obligations...
about the goals
you're working toward
and the boy or girl you're
dreaming of
and the family you belong to...
Do you?

To Ask Yourself

Where did you go
What have you seen
Was the sunlight warming, the gulls' cry still sad
Did the children seem charming
Were the roads picturesque
Did they lead you past cabins, through daisy
    fields in spring
And along rugged foothills, all pine-treed, steep-
    cliffed
What caught your eye
Whose worn face appealed
When you turned that last corner, what made
    your heart sing
Was it smooth and pied-pebbled
Or squat mushrooms rain-swelled
Did you hear your own echo
Did the wind whistle the wires
Were you swept along beaches all sand-shined
    and clean
Had you wandered from familiars into streets
    with strange names
Or were you new awakened till old sights
    seemed sweet
Would you go there again
What quaint-cornered custom would you claim
    for your own
What did you learn
Where e'r you went
What did you see
With your eyes
Heaven sent?

Some of the special things I've seen:

_____

_____

_____

_____

_____

_____

_____

_____

_____

_____

_____

_____

_____

_____

_____

_____

_____

_____

_____

_____

_____

_____

_____

ABOUT THE UGLY UGLIES

Ugly uglies are the other side of life. As you live you may see things you never want to see again.

You may hear words that you wish you hadn't, words that offend and spoil and degrade.

You may be given a reading assignment in school with graphic descriptions focused on the rotting side of reality.

Life presents us the ugly uglies, too, but

Why dwell on the ugly uglies?

Why be preoccupied with thoughts, words, situations, that aren't lifting to your soul?

Instead, consider the ugly uglies as a very small and very sad segment of life.

Pray for help in erasing from your mind the impact of the ugly uglies.

Remember, all life isn't like that and everybody is not involved in the uglies.

You are not—by choice!

Things I can do to make the world a better place:

_____

_____

_____

_____

_____

_____

_____

_____

_____

_____

_____

_____

_____

_____

_____

_____

_____

_____

_____

_____

_____

_____

_____

_____

_____

ABOUT GIVING CREDIT

Find a new way to make a fuss over your friends: a snappy serenade, a surprise chorale, a friendly songfest. It's something your crowd can do to bring fun into your own lives and great delight into the heart of the lucky person who deserves some credit and gets serenaded by you and your crowd.

Here's how the idea works. Someone gets a special honor—could be a birthday, but think of other occasions like: teen of the week, outstanding girl in your school, high scorer at the game, speech contest winner, star in the play or recital, new owner of a driver license. Slyly check to see if the person's home, then round up the group and trot in the direction of your friend's home. When your award-winning friend answers your knock, you start the chant. It can be "for he's a jolly good fellow." Present a huge certificate (made by you?) of achievement. Take along a box of candy, cookies, popcorn, donuts, or an evergreen and ribbon lei . . . and your sweetest smiles, your friendliest manners. Spread a little sunshine, giving credit where credit is due.

People we've honored—why and how:

_____

_____

_____

_____

_____

_____

_____

_____

_____

_____

_____

_____

_____

_____

_____

_____

_____

_____

_____

_____

_____

_____

_____

_____

_____

_____

_____

_____

_____

ABOUT BEGINNINGS AND ENDINGS

To every thing there is a season, . . . A time to be born, and a time to die."

So we read in Ecclesiastes.

Everyone is somewhere along the way between our beginning and our end.

You know the time of the one—your birthday is special.

No one knows the other—but it will come.

Until then, this is your season. This is your day.

This is the time the Lord has made for you.

It is his gift.

What you do in your season largely depends on how you handle your particular happenings. The choice in life is not—it is *not*—between fame and failure, money and poverty, beauty or ugliness. It is not even between passing and failing an exam, or whether you are invited to the homecoming dance or not. The big choice is between good and evil, right and wrong, smart and stupid. The choice is all yours. You are the author of your own book of Acts, writer of your script, star of your season.

Though you can't predict the end, you can make choices that move you from an innocent beginning to a righteous end, whenever it comes.

It helps to find out what you believe, what you know for certain, and what you hold most valuable. Ask yourself some questions like: How do you feel about life—its social, spiritual, physical aspects? What do you believe about religion, total honesty, marriage, people, dating, life after death, keeping the Sabbath day holy, drinking, gossip, freedom, classroom cheating, helping or being helped, chastity, paying debts, assuming responsibility? These are important in your life. Consider them carefully. Which ones are worth standing up for? How important are they to your future, your happiness, to others? How do your ideals, your philosophies, differ from or support your parents' views, friends' views, Heavenly Father's guidelines?

This is only a beginning, but it can help your ending.

Choices I've made between right and wrong:

_____

_____

_____

_____

_____

_____

_____

_____

_____

_____

_____

_____

_____

_____

_____

_____

_____

_____

_____

_____

_____

_____

_____

_____

_____

_____

_____

ABOUT HERE AND THERE

*L*ife is a school and not a reward.

We have to learn how to make our heaven before we can live in it.

These thoughts might help you here and hereafter:

Youthful You

You . . .
make all the difference to . . .
    a play
    a game
    a youth conference
    a festival
    a church outing
    a service project
    a fireside
    a class party

By your very presence *you* make all the difference. Everybody really is there. But it isn't just the fact of the more the merrier. It's that *you* add a quality nobody else can. You've already learned to be socially smart and personally responsive. You are interested and caring and enthusiastic and absolutely alive. You realize your responsibility as a guest or a participant to rise to the occasion envisioned by the host or sponsoring committee. Such qualities spell success for a function. But being on the scene isn't really enough. It's being there every moment. Since you are that kind of person, youthful *you* make all the difference.

Savoring

Plenty of people go through life
grabbing and gulping
everything from food to experiences.
We've been conditioned by quick-food lines
and disposable goods
with everything tasting like
the package it comes in.
Cardboard is synonymous
with grabbing and gulping.
Life is one big Twinkie!
To some.
But not for you...hmmm?
Selecting, feeling, knowing
Savoring.
Put life back into life
gratitude back into good times
value back into possessions
meaning back into relationships
love back into love.
Mmmm...Savoring.
Something to learn how to do.

Patience

Patience is another name for
The waiting game.
You wait to get your ears pierced
to drive
or for your first kiss.
All nature is proof of patience
the butterfly from the cocoon
the peach from the blossom
the leaf from the dry twig
the bird from the egg
spring after winter storms.
It takes a lifetime to make a tree.
And until the girl becomes a woman
it takes patience.
If you can wait until your birthday
without peeking and poking the presents
If you can relish the time you're in
instead of rushing the schedule, tampering with
God's agenda for your life
You'll be surprised how quickly
patience
pays off.
The waiting game is worth it.
In Philippians 4:11 we read,
"for I have learned, in whatsoever
state I am, therewith to be content."

What Matters Most

What matters most
shouldn't be shoved
aside by
what matters least.
Should it?
Consider
what matters most to you
and why.
Then
consider
what you are willing to do
to protect and preserve your values
in life.

"Abstinence makes the heart grow fonder,"
Someone has said.
It's a great slogan for
today's instant-gratification crowd
who may not know
what matters most.
And remember, anticipation can
outclass instant gratification.

Some things I hold as special about life here and there:

_____
_____
_____
_____
_____
_____
_____
_____
_____
_____
_____
_____
_____
_____
_____
_____
_____
_____
_____
_____
_____
_____
_____
_____
_____
_____
_____
_____

ABOUT QUESTIONING
AND UNDERSTANDING

Why do I behave as I do?

Why do other people act as they do? ("Other" people are what we often call adamant parents, jealous peers, wayward friends, self-seeking singles, sour senior citizens, cold executives, unreasonable teachers, wishy-washy religionists, demanding employers, confusing "steadies"!)

How does anybody get everything all figured out?

Where are the answers?

Who has the real knowledge from God?

Why is life like it is?

What's in it for me, anyway?

What happens, really, if I blow it?

Will I always be as I am now?

Is anybody really happy?

Tennyson says:

> Flower in the crannied wall,
> I pluck you out of the crannies,
> I hold you here, root and all, in my hand,
> Little flower—but *if* I could understand
> What you are, root and all, and all in all,
> I should know what God and man is.
> ("Flower in the Crannied Wall")

Consider these qualities:

Would you tell your parents the practice was over at ten o'clock when it was really over at nine-thirty?

If you broke your mother's favorite vase, would you admit it?

Would you fib a little to avoid controversy?

Have you done something helpful for others lately?

Would you withhold information in a bishop's interview?

Would you tell a clerk who gave you too much change?

You wouldn't steal a watermelon from a store— would you from a farmer's field? Is there a difference?

Do you believe "finders, keepers" if the item is something you really want?

Would you take credit you didn't deserve?

This is how I feel about questioning:

_____
_____
_____
_____
_____
_____
_____
_____
_____
_____
_____
_____
_____
_____
_____
_____
_____
_____
_____
_____
_____
_____
_____
_____
_____
_____

♥　　♥　　♥　　♥　　♥　　♥　　♥

ABOUT SPEAKING
ALPHABETICALLY

Apples are for polishing. They're people-pleasers. So are kind looks and gentle phrases.

Balls are for bouncing in sing-alongs and volley games. People with bounce get around more, too.

Clocks are for ticking and tocking. Some people are like clocks—they make things tick with their talking.

Doing is what comes naturally to those who have boned up on gracious behavior already.

Eyes are for eyeing the beauties about—like the eyes of a friend and the dew in the dawn.

Fun is for having.

Girls are for giving, goodness, gladness, growth.

Hearts and hearths and hands and houses are nicest when they're warm and welcoming.

Ideas are for getting.

Jobs are for finishing well—school jobs, church jobs, home jobs, job jobs.

Kisses are for keeping until the real thing comes along.

Love is to give and to take at the right time in the right way.

Mothers are for appreciating.

Noises are for listening to, like night birds, anthems, foghorns, canoe paddles, toe tappers, and the intricate idiom of new music.

Obedience is for teens who want to honor their parents, that their days may be long on the land that the Lord has given them.

P is for people and places and patterns of living that give delight in all their differences.

Quiet is for savoring.

Remembering is for lonely nights in one's own wilderness. It's sweeter when memories are memorable.

Smiles are for sharing. Smiles are for spreading sunshine. Smiles are for making anyone better looking.

Truth is for telling.

Understanding is for trying times. It's for parents and children and teachers and everyone.

Virtue is indeed its own reward.

Watching is for the smart ones—watching pace-setters, fashion trends, and your step. Some-one is watching you, too. Look out!

X marks the spot where you are. Where do you go from here?

Youth is for having once in a lifetime. Cherish it.

Zzzzzzzz makes you sleepy. But are you going to zzzz your life away?

Alphabetically speaking, these are some of my favorite words:

ABOUT SOCIAL PRESSURE

Someday, sooner or later, somebody is going to offer you a drink. Somebody will coax you to try a cigarette. Somebody will taunt you to get stoned. Somebody will jeer until you step up the car speed, or step down to his moral level. Somebody will plead for an answer from you during exams. And somebody just might scoff at your devotion to God.

And what are you going to do about it?

Emerson said, "It is easy in the world to live after the world's opinion; it is easy in solitude to live after our own. But the great man is he who in the midst of the crowd keeps with perfect sweetness the independence of solitude."

How can you withstand the social pressures that
go against the grain of your special life?

Make up your mind ahead of time. Consider
why you have the standards you do.

Have ready answers. Clever, interesting, fun but
firm things to reply when given an offer to
lower your standards in any way.

Act with confidence. You may be nervous or
embarrassed or even frightened, but don't
let it show.

Change the subject. Refuse to take such a
foolish offer seriously. Quickly move on to
another subject.

Having done all ... *stand. Withstand!*

*No matter how much you are teased, tempted,
taunted, coaxed, laughed at, or pleaded with,
remember who you are and what you want for your
own life.*

About What Comes Next

What do you do
when you've done it all
already
and what do you do when
everybody else is doing
what nobody probably ought to be doing
anyway?
What dangerous, thwarting
illegal thing do you do
for the good time—
and then
what comes next?

What I say when I want to say no:

_____

_____

_____

_____

_____

_____

_____

_____

_____

_____

_____

_____

_____

_____

_____

_____

_____

_____

_____

_____

_____

_____

_____

_____

ABOUT MAKING MISTAKES

*I*f you have made a

mistake
and
don't correct it
you are making
another
mistake.

About Handshakes

It's an international custom to shake hands.
It's a gracious tradition. It's something you'll
begin doing in your new grown-up world. Consider what Helen Keller once said:

> The hands of those I meet are dumbly eloquent to me.
> The touch of some hands is an impertinence. I have
> met people so empty of joy that when I clasped their
> frosty fingertips it seemed as if I were shaking hands
> with a northeast storm. Others there are whose hands
> have sunbeams in them, so that their grasp warms my
> heart.

And let that be a sweet lesson to you about
handshaking.

About a Can of Worms

You know the outside ought to reflect the inside. A can of crab labeled crushed pineapple is still a can of crab. It would be great in a soufflé but not on ice cream! It becomes the proverbial "can of worms." You can fool a lot of people a lot of the time, but it just might not be to your advantage. Better to look like what you are and be what you ought to be.

Other bits of wisdom I like:

_____
_____
_____
_____
_____
_____
_____
_____
_____
_____
_____
_____
_____
_____
_____
_____
_____
_____
_____
_____
_____
_____
_____
_____
_____
_____
_____

ABOUT MISSILES
BY MAIL

Here's something you
can do for the love of it.
Here's something you can do for the fun of it.
Here's something you can do for somebody else,
    expecting exactly nothing in return.
You can launch missiles by mail to those away
    from home.

A Long Letter...

   Tote a roll of cash-register tape with you to
various gatherings and fill it with messages
written by friends of the person away.

Thoughts for Each Day...

   Do some thumbing through publications for
happy, inspiring thoughts and poetry. Perhaps
include clever cartoons. Record these and mail
one a day.

Good Goodies...

   Stir up some cookies that won't crumble, and
candy that will keep till it arrives, and package
in gaily decorated gift boxes.

Pocket-book Editions . . .

Let imagination take over while you create a digest of local happenings, mount on colored-paper squares and bind together with yarn or ribbon. Scribble descriptive notes alongside programs—bits of decor, meeting details.

Photo Album . . .

You and your camera might not come forth with award-winning photos each time, but when the models are the favorite people at home your long-gone friend will think you're the greatest.

Clipping Service . . .

Train your eye (and your heart) to follow the news with a twofold purpose—once for you and once for clippings the person away will enjoy.

Proxy Party . . .

When it's a birthday time or congratulations are in order for something else, round up friends and stage a party. Could be a sock or hankie shower. Have everyone make a card, help decorate, and fill the box. Mail this missile to the person away from home.

Writing Right

The art of letter writing should be cultivated because ours is a society demanding many kinds of correspondence. It's good to know what is proper so you represent yourself well.

Writing right proves one's willingness to comply with accepted rules of a civilized society, to be polite. Writing right is kindly, flattering, and pleasing to others. Writing right gives a proper impression of the writer. Writing right brings better results.

Since a letter speaks for you, be aware of the importance of legible handwriting and correct grammar, punctuation, and spelling. Use of a dictionary can improve your technique and style.

Let's consider the right letter for the right time:

1. Thank-you notes—write simple and sincere notes of appreciation as soon as you can after a kindness has been shown you.
2. Casual correspondence—write as if you were talking to someone. Remember that written material is more lasting than spoken words, so write accordingly.
3. Letters of invitation—when you are responsible to invite a speaker or soloist for a special event, be formal in paper, style, and content. Double check to see if all needful details are included. Let your language be respectful and appreciative.

Names and addresses of new friends, old acquaintances, etc.:

_____

_____

_____

_____

_____

_____

_____

_____

_____

_____

_____

_____

_____

_____

_____

_____

_____

_____

_____

_____

_____

_____

_____

_____

_____

_____

♥ ♥ ♥ ♥ ♥ ♥ ♥

ABOUT YOUR
CHOICE GENERATION

You are part of a choice generation—that generation born that much closer to the second coming of Christ

trained up in the way you should go by new methods to help you learn better, faster

owner of more personal property and equipment (electronic and sports) than any generation before you

aware of the real meaning of the brotherhood of man

tolerant and accepting of people who are different from you in belief, in nationality, in political thinking, in economic or educational opportunities

groomed and bred by the best in health care

You are self-starting and ambitious to improve. You invest your humanity informally, grandly or simply as the situation demands. And you study. College entrance being competitive these days, grades and qualifying have a big place in your life.

So there you are—intelligent, beautiful, studious, spiritual, tolerant, socially smart. There is another area to applaud you—you believe. God is a part of your life. Your faith is less blind than your parents' faith. Your life hasn't been so sheltered and you make your choices out of comparison, with knowledge, with confidence. As a result, you understand more about repentance than past generations your age. You do what is right not just out of duty or obedience but because you've considered the alternative.

Many young people in the world today aren't blessed with your kind of understanding about life. They don't understand about life before this and life after this and how life now fits in between. They think they invented free agency and attitudes about over-population and personal rights. They think they are the only ones who abhor war, and yet they'll tolerate violence on the streets.

You are a choice generation because of your timing in the scheme of things but never forget that your own agency to choose, to act, to resist, to contribute, has a great deal to do with your being noteworthy, too.

So, choose to stay choice.

About Pericles and You

In ancient days Pericles stood on a hill over-looking Athens and said, "I see Athens not for what she is but for what she may become."

And what can you become?

You can grow mentally, physically, spiritually, socially.

But you need time to meditate, time to play and train and compete.

You need to participate and express yourself, to improve your mind and strengthen character, to develop talents and learn leadership and social skills, to increase your understanding of God, to serve others, to discipline self, to search and stretch and persist in doing. You need work to do, and times for enduring, sacrificing, loving. You want to get good at effectively meeting frustration, temptation. You need to identify yourself with significant goals, make a commitment to God—his kingdom and his cause.

It isn't what you are now that will mark you forever—it's what you'll become!

What I want to be like someday:

♥　♥　♥　♥　♥　♥　♥

ABOUT PUTTING OUT THE FIRE

*I*t's great that you're smarter than the adults you see all around you smoking their health and their money away. Of course, when they were your age, they didn't know what you know about the troubles that go with smoking.

Since you don't smoke, be a good friend and help others to withstand brainwashings, advertisements, and temptings of all kinds that lead to smoking. Make yours a smokeless generation! Here are some good reasons why:

1. Smoking is contrary to the revealed word of God. He knows what is for our best good.
2. The evidence is overwhelming that smoking is dangerous, disabling, frequently fatal.
3. It is expensive and offensive.
4. It is discourteous.
5. It enslaves.

Honestly, there isn't a single redeeming factor about smoking—except for the tobacco companies.

Here's a Personal Code of Clean Living

It's great to be young, to feel fit for fun and for the rewarding pursuits of our world. With just one chance to live, I would make of it a superior experience. I would value my life, my mind, my body; not take unto me any unclean, unwise, or unhealthy thing that might weaken my will, dull my senses, or in any way impair my physical or moral potential. I would withstand social pressures, realizing full well that "just this once" can become a lifetime habit. I know that *everybody* is *not* smoking. I'm not!

Here's a Tribute to You

Some people insist upon stating what's wrong with today's youth. But actually there is much that is right with you. You get higher grades, go to church more, eat fewer sweets, serve better, travel farther, think more deeply, have firm opinions of your own, know more about your country and current affairs, spend more and shop better, play more but study more, too, than your counterparts of other years.

You are on-the-go, creative, tongue-in-cheek creatures who delight in unnerving parents and leaders with far-out fads, new ideas, and commitments to an unfamiliar cause. But beneath an appearance that may be shocking to adults, there are hearts searching for the good, for truth, for values that rest well on the conscience.

Yours is a grown-up generation, one to be reckoned with. You earn higher wages and boast more talent skills than any other age group in history. A small percentage of you are termed "delinquent" and often color the case for all the rest, getting media coverage and the blasts from parents. But the remaining many go quietly along preparing to take the torch for our tomorrows.

My own reasons for clean living:

_____
_____
_____
_____
_____
_____
_____
_____
_____
_____
_____
_____
_____
_____
_____
_____
_____
_____
_____
_____
_____
_____
_____
_____
_____
_____
_____

ABOUT THE BARD AND YOU

Shakespeare had this to say about youth: "...youth, ripe for exploits and mighty enterprises." Let's take Shakespeare at his word and get on with the mighty enterprise, the big exploit of making the most out of what we have to work with. Herewith a program of self-improvement, Shakespeare style.

Act I Romeo and Juliet
Boy meets girl needn't be a lamentable tragedy.

Shakespeare says about girls:

> ...but the full sum of me...
> Is an unlesson'd girl, unschool'd, unpractised:
> Happy in this, she is not yet so old
> But she may learn; happier than this,
> She is not bred so dull but she can learn.
> (The Merchant of Venice)

Shakespeare says about boys:

> ...O, it is excellent
> To have a giant's strength; but it is tyrannous
> To use it like a giant.
> (Measure for Measure)

We say:

Learn. Live by your learning well, using all your gifts wisely.

Act II The Taming of the Shrew
Self-control is the basis of popularity.

Shakespeare says about behavior:

> Love thyself last; cherish those hearts that hate thee;
> Corruption wins not more than honesty
> Still in thy right hand carry gentle peace,
> To silence envious tongues. Be just, and fear not:
> (King Henry the Eighth)

We say:

Listen to your leaders who can help you behave better, learn more; remember how to be socially smart, morally straight, physically fit, and spiritually awakened.

Act III The Comedy of Errors
Some mix-ups aren't so merry!

Shakespeare says:

> ...to thine own self be true;
> And it must follow as the night the day,
> Thou canst not then be false to any man.
> (Hamlet)

We say:

Some people look like what they aren't and aren't what they look like. Be the best of whatever you are.

Act IV Much Ado About Nothing

Shakespeare says:

> Beauty itself doth of itself persuade
> The eyes of men without an orator.
> ("Lucrece")

We say:

Lots of teens make much ado about nothing and forget that real beauty is inside.

Act V All's Well That Ends Well

Shakespeare says:

> All's well that ends well.
> (All's Well That Ends Well)

We say:

Live each day as if it were at once the end of your life and the beginning. Improve on your past; live the present without regrets; determine to make the future a bright one.

Here's how I've done it:

Act I   The boys and I

_____
_____
_____
_____
_____

Act II   My steps toward self-mastery

_____
_____
_____
_____

Act III   My most embarrassing moment

_____
_____
_____

Act IV   My beauty routine

_____
_____
_____

Act V   The ways I've improved

_____
_____
_____

ABOUT TALKING IT OVER

*I*f talking to your plants works magic, try talking to your parents! In the right time and in the right way such communication can bring desired results.

There is a right time, a better time for everything, including asking for money, getting permission, issuing a complaint, talking things over. Putting it to your parents squarely, you may get some straight answers to some tough questions.

Or you may get a lecture, an awkward silence, a desperate attempt at changing the subject. You may not like what you hear. You may refuse to listen.

Impasse. Nowhere. Frustration for everyone. The generation gap in action.

But keep trying. You're involved here with people who care, who love you—anyway. A sincere grown-up-to-grown-up approach in facing the problems of life can be beneficial to all concerned. Each side of the generation picture tries a little harder to wear the other's glasses. Each assumes the other is a well-meaning, intelligent child of God. Each approaches the task of arriving at agreement on disagreeable subjects with an attitude of appreciation for all the other one is trying to be, for all he really is.

Dad's knowledge and mother's understanding can be powerful helps in the mean wrestle with life. Your fresh learning, positive approach, and simple faith give valuable perspective.

We hear some stern admonishments that youth should "honour thy father and thy mother." What we don't hear often enough and understand fully is the importance of the rest of that scripture: "that thy days may be long upon the land which the Lord thy God giveth thee" (Exodus 20:21).

You want your days to be long, your life to be full. Well, so do your parents! Give them a chance to counsel with you, carefully and prayerfully and patiently learning together. With them consider the value of time-tested, God-given principles as compared with today's trends. What is really important here? What is at stake? Why is sin sinful? Why is unchastity near the top of the list of "thou shalt nots"? Why are drugs dangerous? Why is pornography destroying? What about fads in appearance and behavior? What's right for *your* family? Your kind of people will give you your kind of answer. Talk it over.

Things I'm learning from other people:

_____

_____

_____

_____

_____

_____

_____

_____

_____

_____

_____

_____

_____

_____

_____

_____

_____

_____

_____

_____

_____

_____

_____

_____

_____

ABOUT YOU

We love you, mini-moneyed students, you maxi-hearted luminaries (no mini-spirits, you!), you uptight, earth-bound visionaries, and you who pluck guitar strings, as well as you who make the scenes; you whose fingers boast ten rings, you who work on cars and things. And you who sell, and you who paint, or work with ladies losing weight, or hoe the corn, or sing the songs, or count the cash, or right the wrongs.

We love you . . . every one! All you who tend the stables, control cables, tell kids fables, paint old gables, sew on labels, read of Babel, pitch the ball or just walk tall—we love you . . . every one!

We note with warmth your casual cleanness and your lack of falseness, meanness. You who search in faith with keenness; you with fat and you with leanness—we love you . . . every one!

We love you best for your involvement, you who care about your "neighbor," whatever his race or type or status; for his rights you're quick to labor. You are a heartwarmer.

We love your penchant for authenticity, your sophisticated simplicity, your up-with-change, down-on-duplicity, your *joie de vivre* felicity. We love your big, happy, trying heart—we love you, every one!

People who have warmed my heart:

_____

_____

_____

_____

_____

_____

_____

_____

_____

_____

_____

_____

_____

_____

_____

_____

_____

_____

_____

_____

_____

_____

_____

_____

_____